Wicca

Not Just for Beginners. Part 2 – Continue of the First Very Successful Wicca for Beginners! A Book for Wiccans, Witches and Other Seekers for Magic! Great to Listen in a Car!

© Copyright by Judith Guise 2019 - All rights reserved.

The content contained within this book may not be reproduced, duplicated or transmitted without direct written permission from the author or the publisher.

Under no circumstances will any blame or legal responsibility be held against the publisher, or author, for any damages, reparation, or monetary loss due to the information contained within this book, either directly or indirectly.

Legal Notice:

This book is copyright protected. It is only for personal use. You cannot amend, distribute, sell, use, quote or paraphrase any part, or the content within this book, without the consent of the author or publisher.

Disclaimer Notice:

Please note the information contained within this document is for educational and entertainment purposes only. All effort has been executed to present accurate, up to date, reliable, complete information. No warranties of any kind are declared or implied. Readers acknowledge that the author is not engaging in the rendering of legal, financial, medical or professional advice. The content within this book has been derived from various sources. Please consult a licensed professional before attempting any techniques outlined in this book.

By reading this document, the reader agrees that under no circumstances is the author responsible for any losses, direct or indirect, that are incurred as a result of the use of information contained within this document, including, but not limited to, errors, omissions, or inaccuracies.

Table of Contents

Introduction..5

Chapter 1: Wicca Breakdown....................8

Chapter 2: Self-Care with Wicca................6

Chapter 3: Family and Wicca..................42

Chapter 4: Covens...................................46

Chapter 5: Your Personal Wiccan Journey..60

Chapter 6: Intermediate Spells...............67

Conclusion...95

References...99

Introduction

Thank you for choosing this guide to help further your Wiccan prowess. There is so much to learn in the realm of Wicca that it can seem overwhelming at first. But you have made it through the first steps into the world of Wicca and you are now here trying to advance the knowledge and powers that you have.

Wicca is a continual journey where you will always be working on yourself and your connection to this world. There will be areas that need more focus than others and you might even have a certain affinity for one particular kind of magic than you do for another.

As we all practice our Wiccan beliefs and familiarize ourselves with the religion, there are times when we forget the importance of self-care. As a Wiccan, self-care is incredibly important because you are your own source of natural energy. Remember that Wicca is a religion that focuses on the connection and balance between your spiritual self and nature. If you are worn down, your spiritual self will not be able to strengthen its connection to nature.

The amazing thing about Wicca is that there is no ONE way to practice. You have the ability to cater your beliefs and practices to what suits you on your personal journey in Wicca. Now that you understand the basics, I really want to use this guide to help you focus on your own personal journey within the religion of Wicca. Sometimes we get too lost by concentrating on what we think we should be doing, rather than focusing on how what we are doing is affecting us and our connections with nature.

As a Wiccan you understand that your religion is not the only one in the world, and you embrace the differences that arise not only within the Wiccan community but outside it as well. Wicca is not a religion where shaming another for their beliefs and practices is a concept. That is one of the reasons Wiccans find great community with one another. It is also something that I am going to extensively cover within this guide - the difference between family and covens and how you choose to practice with them.

I am going to add a brief disclaimer that this book is not a cure all for any health issues or concerns. I am not making any grand claims that this guide will cure ailments. I am simply providing you with the tools that you can use to practice self-care and to find your path in Wicca.

I hope that you enjoy the journey you are about to embark on and that you use the tools provided here to strengthen your own personal connection with the world. Let us start with a quick rundown of Wicca before diving into the advanced concepts.

Chapter 1: Wicca Breakdown

Whenever we are diving into a more advanced version of spells and magic than before I like to go back and give a brief recap of what Wicca is and its history. The reason for this is because I believe that it is important to understand the origins of the religion that you are practicing. It might also help you find where you see yourself in this religion.

Today, Wicca is a pagan based religion that concentrates on the believer's connection with nature. It also has a central focus on worshipping the feminine God and the masculine God. However, this was not always what Wicca looked like or stood for. Like many other religions, Wicca has evolved into what it is today through shifting beliefs, ideals, and the passage of time.

Brief Recap of History

If you practice Wicca today and have had some introduction to its origins, then it should come as no surprise to hear the name Margaret Murray. She is often credited as the woman who created the structures for Wicca as it is practiced today.

Murray wrote books regarding how witch cults were formed and witchcraft was practiced in 1920s Britain. Many followers of the Wiccan religion at that time adopted the structure that she described within her books.

It was not until 1954, however, that Wicca finally got its name. Before then, people merely called Wiccan practices witchcraft and sorcery. Gerald Gardner named Wicca, originally spelling it "wica". This word, in Gardner's understanding, was derived from old Scottish English and meant "wise people".

Despite many Wiccan followers using Murray's structure for their covens and practices, Gardner is ultimately considered the father of Wicca. The interesting thing about Wicca today is that it is not built upon any one person, but instead, it has come to exist today through collective beliefs from people such as Margaret Murray, Gerald Gardner, and Aleister Crowley.

Aleister Crowly met Gerald Gardner in 1947 and the pair shared many of the same ideas for what a coven should look and what Wiccan practices meant for the practitioner. *The Book of Shadows* was written by Gardner sometime between 1940 and 1950 and is still considered a staple of Wiccan practices today. However, while Gardner's name rests upon the book, it is important to remember that many people beyond the three mentioned here lent their own beliefs to make up what he wrote.

Doreen Valiente is an important name in Wiccan history as well. She too knew Gardner and they collaborated together to create a revised copy of *The Book of Shadows*. Through conflicts that arose, Valiente ended up breaking away from Gardner's coven and starting her own. Through this many smaller covens were created due to the different ways in which Wicca was practiced.

Through all of these years Wicca's focus was on magic. However, in the 1970's as times changed, Feminism was gaining traction, and Americans were pushing back on environmentalism which caused Wicca's basis to change from magic to a more nature-focused religion. This shift in focus changed the ways that Wicca was practiced both across America and England (where its pagan beliefs were started).

Wicca had its own struggles being recognized as a legitimate religion, and many people scoffed at it or viewed it as devil worship. It was not until 1986 that Wicca was legally a recognized religion that earned it the same legal respect as all other religions. Since 1986 there have been many cases with Wicca making progress as being internationally accepted by schools, prisons, and other institutions. Before Wiccan items were withheld from those who practiced, but now thankfully those who practice have the same rights to their talismans as other religions do.

How Wicca Has Expanded

Wicca's extensive history is full of turmoil and conflict. However, despite its troubled past, Wicca has continued to grow and flourish as a religion. As Wicca grew, more and more people learned about it and were drawn to the ways in which Wicca focused on a person's connection with nature. The other drawing factor was how much acceptance for self and others exists in Wicca.

Wicca was based on beliefs that predated Christian ideals and traditions. And through the years, as it has shaped into the nature-based religion we know today, it has also gained massive popularity. As new generations grow up without the stigma that Wicca used to have, the religion has become more widely accepted and adopted.

In 1990 it was roughly estimated that there were around 8,000 practitioners of the Wicca religion. This may not seem like a lot, but even with missing data in 2008 it was estimated to have grown well over 300,000 practitioners! That is a huge jump within a short amount of time (Kopf, 2018).

While Wicca does have its roots in Pagan beliefs, it is critical to note that Wicca and Paganism are two completely separate belief systems. But Pagan ideals are growing too and match the growth that Wicca has experienced.

More recent studies were run in 2014 regarding how much of the population identifies as Wiccan. The Pew Research Center released data that suggested that as of 2014 over one million people identified as believing in Wicca (Kopf, 2018). That is exponential growth within a short amount of time.

As Wicca has grown in popularity, the conglomerate giants have taken notice. Both the beauty and wellness industries have realized how popular Wicca has become and have started tapping into this previously underdeveloped market. Due to this interest, the rising popularity of mysticism and being "witchy" has grown. Movies and television shows are marketed to tap into this mystic sector.

These thoughts of magic and a connection with nature have been popularized by the beauty and television giants, which have made the idea of being Wiccan a growing concept around millennials.

The bottom line? Wicca continues to grow every single day. With marketing being geared directly toward Wiccans and other mystic believers, these products and ideals reach a wider audience. Wicca has exploded in the twenty-first century, being embraced by many with open arms.

What Wicca Means to You

I have said it before and I will stress it again. Wicca is a personal journey. There are so many different ways to practice and different ideals and beliefs within the Wiccan community that your connection to nature through this religion is your very own personal journey. You get to decide the path it takes and who you let yourself become as you evolve through this journey.

Wicca is not witchcraft, and should not be confused with the derogatory terms that have been used to describe witchcraft in the past. As of today, your Wiccan religion is a true recognized and validated belief system.

The ideas of being Wiccan and being a witch are not mutually exclusive, you can have one without the other, or you can alternatively join them both together. The focus of Wicca is not the practice of magic or witchcraft, but rather how you connect to nature and the universe around you.

Wicca is not a religion for everyone. Let me clarify this point, Wicca can be practiced by anyone. But not everyone will find the sanctuary that they are looking for within Wicca. The great thing about the Wiccan community though is that they are generally very accepting and open to having questions asked, as well as open to teaching others their beliefs.

For you, Wicca is going to take on different paths. This is entirely dependent on how you intend to practice and follow Wicca. At its core though, being Wiccan means that you will worship the female goddess, and at times the male god (this depends on who you most favor for your spells, incantations, and magic). Most people worship the female goddess because she symbolizes life and fertility.

You can practice Wicca for yourself, for your family, and even in a coven setting. Because it is such a personal journey, you will have to define for yourself how you view Wicca and what it means to you. For most people, Wicca is a stronger connection to nature.

You will find that most Wiccans practice veganism or are even vegetarian. For those that do not, they are more careful with their meat consuming practices. They are also intensely aware of the impact that this world is having on the natural environment.

Wicca is a religion where you can find light and solace. As long as you keep making progress on yourself, you are evolving within Wicca. The goal is to always be a kinder, gentler, and more understanding version of yourself.

If you are new to Wicca and are reading this, I urge you to throw away all previous misconceptions that you might have had about what Wicca is and what it means. Allow yourself to connect with the Wiccan religion with a new perspective and open mind. You might just find that it fills you and changes you in ways that you never believed possible - and this is all for good.

Chapter 2: Self-Care with Wicca

This is the biggest part of this guide, because it is also one of the most critical parts. Self-care is essential to you as a Wiccan. There are no shortcuts with this, and burnout will only be detrimental to you in the long run.

The purpose of practicing self-care in Wicca is so that you can enhance the quality of your life. This includes the natural and mystical parts of your practice. There are some key concepts when it comes to practicing self-care in Wicca and certain parts of the body and mind that Wicca pays close attention to. In this chapter we will be exploring what parts of the body and mind that you need to care for, especially when you are hoping to strengthen your natural connection to this world.

Meditation with Wicca

Meditation is a necessary part of your Wiccan craft, and it is hard to center yourself or strengthen your connection to nature when you fail to practice your meditation. Meditation does not always have to be what you have been traditionally exposed to. This means that you can find your meditative techniques through more than just sitting cross-legged.

When you are able to take stock of the world around you and focus on the connections you have made with nature you will find that you meditate far more often than you were consciously aware of. The purpose of meditation within Wicca is to further your own personal journey and to provide you with wisdom. If you want, you can meditate with other objects, you can focus on energy transferring between you and another object, you can focus on the peace that you get from a specific object as well. If you find that drawing, gardening or even cleaning gets you into a calm and meditative state then you are welcome to explore those avenues as well.

When you are first trying to meditate, I recommend that you find an area where you are going to be quiet and undisturbed. Oftentimes I will recommend that you search for a place in nature before trying out any other avenues. This is because nature is going to be where you are your strongest and where you feel your calmest.

Make sure that you are in a place where you feel comfortable and in a relaxed position. Take deep breaths and steady yourself through your breathing. For a moment do not think of anything but yourself and your breathing.

Once you have settled into a calm state you should let your mind focus solely on your breathing and the effect that your breathing is having on your body. Don't worry about life in this moment. Let your connection to nature guide you and control you as you meditate. Let the calming surroundings carry into your body. Your muscles will begin to relax and so will you. You will benefit from this.

I like to say that meditation is a technique that should be practiced every single day if possible. Sometimes this is not possible, but even in your quiet moments or if you are sitting in line waiting for something, close your eyes and focus on your breathing. It will make you feel ten times better to get some meditating done every day and give you a renewed vigor to tackle the day with.

Personal Self-Care

The body is a temple. You have probably heard this phrase many times before practiced in conjunction with many other religions. However, in Wicca this phrase is not meant to repress like it is used in other religions. Normally, when you hear the phrase the body is a temple, you might think that you cannot eat anything unhealthy or mark your body with tattoos. That is not the case with Wicca.

When we say that the body is a temple, we talk about the conscious choices of how we choose to care for our bodies both externally and internally. Many Wiccans express themselves through their hair, makeup, and even the tattoos that they place on their bodies. This is their way of self-expression and is considered part of their self-care routine.

For a moment, let us focus on what we internally put into our bodies. Most practicing Wiccans avoid unnatural drugs as they are detrimental to the body. Since the body is such an important source of energy for the Wiccan, they prefer not to deplete that source by consuming harmful drugs. The risk of damaging their sacred temple is too high.

Eating right can be the hardest part of focusing on your internal body self-care. However, this is also a critical part of self-care and cannot be ignored or avoided, nor should it be. Making different choices with eating can occur on a gradual scale or you can do it cold turkey. Remember this is a personal journey, so at the end of the day it truly depends on what you think is the best path for yourself.

One of the best things I can recommend is to only eat foods that are natural. When keeping your body temple clean and pure, you want to make sure that you are not filling it with processed sugars, lots of alcohol, or an excess of over-processed and packaged foods. By eating foods that are natural I do not mean stop eating sweets, or sugars. I just mean to change the processed sugars for more natural ones.

Vegan and vegetarian lifestyles are not for everyone, but you can be conscious in the meat that you consume and where you get it from. You do not need to eat a burger patty that consists of 150 different animals. By being conscious of what you are putting in your body, you are practicing internal self-care.

So, eating fresh fruits and vegetables that naturally occur and are grown organically (even better if you grow them yourself) is a step in the right direction. When your temple is properly nourished it benefits so much more than just your body!

The other important part of physical self-care is exercise. I am not saying that you need to go out and get a gym membership today, but you need to make sure that you are doing some form of physical exercise. This can be as simple as taking a twenty-minute walk through nature every day. Go to a park, find a natural walkway, get out on a hike. There are numerous different ways that you can get physical exercise to nourish your body. The reason

I suggest nature walks as a top priority is because being within and amongst nature is akin to being in a "church-like" setting for Wiccans. Your connection to nature is one of the most important things to a Wiccan.

Aside from your body, taking care of your mind is critical. Meditation is one of the purest and most helpful forms of protecting your mind and making sure that it is well cared for. Meditation helps calm the mind and soul, and it also increases your ability to focus. Focus is crucial to Wiccans because it will help in how effective your incantations and spells are. You will also find that your spirit is fed through your meditation.

The third important aspect that you want to pay attention to when it comes to self-care is your spirit. Mind, body, and spirit make up your temple. The spirit is constantly evolving as you grow within Wicca. When you practice magic, it should be for your own personal growth, not for monetary gain or quests for power. When you are pure and selfless in your intentions, you will find that your personal power will be strongest. Your spirit feeds this personal power.

Your spirit is invigorated through several methods, some of these including but not limited to meditating, conducting self-care rituals, and holding circles. There are other methods, but these are the easiest and most commonly used methods of making sure that your spirit is centered and growing through the guidance of the god and goddess.

There is no Wicca without self-care. Remember that. You need to make sure that you are taking care of yourself and practicing all of these different self-care tactics. You want to be the epitome of health. As your mind, body, and spirit flourish so too will your connection to nature.

Self-Care with Herbs

Below I have compiled some self-care herbal spells that are meant to bring you a greater sense of healing for any pain, deeper connections, as well as a better understanding of your personal self.

Sometimes working with herbs can be daunting, but you do not have to be a master herbalist in order to make use of the benefits of herbal spells. You can even just learn the properties of one or two herbs that you will use consistently and often as you slowly expand your knowledge of herbs. It is important to begin some type of relationship with herbs and other plants as this strengthens your connection to the natural world.

I will highlight a few magical properties of the most popular herbs so that you can begin familiarizing yourself with them:

- Basil - wards off negative energy within a home, brings love into an environment, serves as protection

- Chamomile - relieves stress and tension, brings in love, promotes healing

- Dandelion - closeness to spirits, aids in divination, helps in wishes and wishful thinking

- Lavender - promotes peace and sleep, aids in meditation, helps with healing and protection, offers relief from sadness

- Rosemary - helps with matters of the heart and lust, also works to promote peaceful sleep and rest

While there are many other herbs that you will come into contact with, these are the most common that you will use in self-care routines. When you begin to learn how they can help you and your connection to nature grows, you will find it easier to navigate herbal spells. You might find that you begin to write your own as well.

Restful Tea

Sleep makes a huge difference in the way that we function. It impacts every aspect of our lives, and so it is important to be rested. Nightmares can plague our dreams, restlessness can keep us up late at night, and insomnia can be lurking around the corner waiting to jump on you. This spell offers a quick and calming ritual that will aid your sleeping habits with the use of a simple herb.

The ingredients you will need are:

- Chamomile tea
- Lavender (any form will do but oil or dried leaves work best).

Directions:

1. This spell can vary depending on what form of lavender you have. If your lavender is in a liquid form take a few drops and dab some onto your pillowcase. However, if you have lavender in flowers, simply break off a stalk and place it inside your pillowcase where you will rest your head as you sleep.

2. You will need to boil the water for your tea. It is imperative however that you use no sugar or honey with your tea, leave the tea in its purest form.

3. If you can, sit on your bed and cross your legs one over the other. If this position is too hard for you, you can merely cross your legs together without pulling one on top of the other.

4. Slowly focus on your breathing. Feel every movement inside your chest as you breathe in and then breathe out. When you breathe out, focus on the muscles that are relaxed and feel the tension move out from each muscle that you are releasing, then breathe in again. If there are any issues that are plaguing you or stresses in your life, just picture them as a big black cloud looming in front of you. As you breathe in, focus on taking a deep inhale. When you breathe out, imagine all of that black cloudy darkness being blown away and a white peace replacing it. Let the healing and calming white fill your body and take away the black cloud. Do this a few times until you start to feel your body warm up from the healing white light.

5. As your body warms up and you start to feel a calmness settle over you, close your eyes and imagine yourself not on a bed, but instead sitting in a patch of sunshine in a wooded area. It can be quiet, dappled sunlight that you are picturing, but make

sure that the area you are in is filled with nature. Let the smell of pine needles, soil, and new grass fill your nose. Let the bird song and the chatter of the woodland animals fill your ears. Relax as you transport yourself into this serene environment.

6. Do all of this meditating and imaging as the water for your tea boils. Keep it up until your kettle whistles or you hear the tea boiling. After it has boiled, slowly bring yourself out of your meditation and make a cup of chamomile tea. As the tea steams, breathe this white energy in. Let the smell of the chamomile overwhelm your senses. Hold onto the cup for warmth. As you do this, you should feel your body being calm.

7. Don't gulp your tea down but drink it slowly and thoughtfully. Focus on your peaceful energy, and don't dwell on the black cloud that you blew away. Make sure that you are disconnected from all social media or electronics during this time too. The point of this spell is to turn your body peacefully off, not keep it going.

8. Once the tea is finished, go to bed. Lay your head down by the lavender scent that you had placed on your pillow earlier. While you

are breathing in the lavender scent, allow your muscles and body a chance to relax. Don't feel compelled to move them. Picture yourself resting amongst nature, the gentle hum of life in the trees and plants around you lulling you to sleep.

Healing Hands

Sometimes we feel discouraged in life and it can be hard to get up every morning in the face of insurmountable pain (both physical and mental). This spell is for those who need some help to heal themselves and protect themselves from more harm.

Ingredients to have on hand:

- Bay leaves - signify strength
- Mint leaves - signify vitality
- Sea salt - signifies being cleansed
- Tiger's Eye Stone - signifies protection
- Carnation flower petals
- Incense (sage is best)
- A small square piece of white cloth

- Holy Water
- Two candles that are white
- Dirt from the Earth

Directions:

1. Meditation, as always, is important to include here so that you are able to focus as you cast this spell. It is important because this spell draws on a lot of energy and will sap your strength if you do not adequately prepare for it.

2. Take the square piece of white cloth and write your name down in the middle of the cloth. Once you have written your name down cast your circle.

3. On your altar, spread the white cloth out so that it is open and place the elements around it. These elements will be the holy water, the dirt, sage incense and one of the white candles. Each of these represents earth, air, fire, and water. Make sure not to lose track of all of your ingredients, you will need them shortly.

4. Now you need to repeat the below incantation as you add the following items onto the cloth: the tiger's eye stone, sea salt, the bay leaves, the mint, and the flower

petals. Add each ingredient until you feel like you have added the right amount. Say these words:

"It is with love in me that I call upon the god and goddess,

And all the elementals that I know

Water, Fire, Earth, and Air

And all the power that rests within me

Help me overcome this obstacle in my life,

Bring my health back to where it once was

This is my will, so mote it be."

5. Once you are done with the incantation and adding the necessary ingredients, tie the cloth together until it resembles a sachet. Charge it with your positive energy and think healing thoughts into it. Lay the sachet out under moonlight every single night right after you charge it. It needs to be charged every night as you get ready to sleep. When you feel healed, bury the sachet within the earth around your home and offer this up as an offering to all the forces that came together to bring you health.

Healing or Protection Powder

This powder does wonders for those who need healing in their life from emotional pain, and even for those who are just seeking protection. The great part about practicing magic is that your intentions and energies go into your magic, and that can make all the difference with your spell work.

Ingredients needed:

- A mortar and pestle
- A sharp needle
- Spoon
- A medium-sized bowl
- A velvet sachet or even a small tin (this is where you will store the powder once it is completed).
- Anise seeds
- Chamomile
- Fennel
- Rosemary
- Jasmine flowers
- Star Anise

- Basil leaves

Directions:

1. Using your mortar and pestle, take each root or herb or seed that is on your list and grind them down into a fine powder. It will take some elbow grease on some of them but grind them down as finely as you can. With each grind, focus on the spell that you are about to cast and what your purpose for this spell is. There are other methods of grinding that might appeal to you, but doing it by hand with the mortar and pestle will add to the energy of the spell.

2. There are no specific measurements for the herbs that you are going to use, just add what feels right to you. This is where familiarizing yourself with the herbs helps because then you develop a connection with them. Once you have finished grinding each herb down into a powder, you need to place each powder into the bowl. Don't grind each herb all at once, take your time and grind them down individually. Then, using your spoon mix the different powders together in the bowl to get them nicely blended.

3. Once all the herbs are blended together take the needle and prick your finger gently so that you draw just a few drops of blood. Spill this blood into the mixed powder that you

have ground down. As your blood mingles in with the powder chant:

"Through spirits both new and old that have created wisdom in this world,

Through the blessed goddess and her love and grace,

Through my own diving power and gifts that the goddess has lent to me,

I beckon all these powers to come together, including those of the elements

I beckon you to bless the powder which I have labored to make,

Bless into the powder the ability to achieve my goals and desires,

Bless into it protection and purification and healing,

Allow the powder to be able to find balance through the clouds in this world

May this be done by my will and might,

let it be known through darkness and light

So shall it be in the heavens above us,

So shall it be in the world beneath us.

So mote it be."

4. Once the incantation is done and you have blended in all the necessary ingredients, you need to let the powder dry. Give it time to completely dry out, patience will work in your favor with this spell. Once it is dry add it into either a velvet bag or a small tin will work just as well alternatively.

5. You need to keep the powder with you, and anytime you need it just take out a small dash of the powder and sprinkle it over the flame of a white candle. This will help promote the healing and health that you are seeking.

Self-Care Magic

You don't have to use herbs and incantations in order to find self-care, but they do help. There are other rituals and spells that you can do that will work just as well as the above-mentioned spells that use herbs. That is the brilliant thing about Wicca, there are millions of different ways to practice it and yield the same result.

Peaceful, Healing Bath Time

You will need:

- Warm to hot bath water, fill as much as desired.
- Two tablespoons of olive oil
- Sage leaves
- Four green candles

Directions:

1. In each corner of the bathtub, or even just around the bathtub place one candle. Do not light it yet, just make sure that each side has a candle in place.

2. As you pour hot water into your bathtub drop in the olive oil.

3. Once the bath is full, add your sage leaves while chanting:

   "Through this healing waters I free myself from the entanglements that shadow me.

   So be my will, so mote it be."

4. Light the candles as you finish the incantation and then slide into your bath and relax for at least twenty minutes. You

can meditate while in the bath, or you can just be still. But don't let worries or concerns come into your mind during this time.

Energizing Spell

Ingredients:

- White Candle
- Rose Petals
- Thumbtack or needle to carve
- Star oil (will add the ingredients for this in the directions below)

Directions:

1. To make star oil you will need the following: 10 drops of lemon oil, 7 drops of rosemary oil, 7 drops of jasmine oil, 17 drops of chamomile oil, 5 drops of sandalwood oil. Mix the oils together and you have star oil.

2. Take your white candle, and carve your name into the wax of the candle. Then take your time and carefully anoint the candle with the star oil that you have just made. Charge the candle as you anoint it with desires for energy and health.

3. Sprinkle rose petals on and around the candle, and light the candle. Make sure that you do this only under a waxing moon though. When you burn the candle, you should say the following words:

"Earth, Air, Water, and Fire, give me Protection and Health, it is all I desire"

4. Allow the candle to burn out completely, don't save any of it. Then you should start seeing your desired effects shortly.

Caring for Your Household

Sometimes we are not able to care for ourselves when we know that our home or our family members are in distress. This can be a particularly difficult time for a Wiccan who is in dire need of self-care. Taking care of your household is part of taking care of yourself because it affords you the peace of mind that you need in order to continue your own self-care rituals and routines.

That is why I am going to give you a few protection spells for your home so that every aspect of your life that you care about is covered.

Car Protection

You will need:

- A white candle
- Energy to visualize
- Rosemary oil (optional)

Directions:

1. Light the candle and stand in front of the vehicle that you want to protect. Then visualize a bubble of light that encompasses the vehicle, and seal this bubble of protection by holding your candle in front of the vehicle steadily.

2. If you want, you can anoint the candle with rosemary oil, this will also strengthen the protection spell.

3. Once you have finished visualizing the bubble of protection let the candle finish burning. If you wish to you can also use a small charm that is hung in the car, let the rosemary oil that has been blessed with the visualization image drop onto the charm as well. The vehicle will now be protected and you can have peace of mind as family members travel in the vehicle with or without you.

Protecting Your Home

You will need:

- Garlic
- Salt

- Rosemary in powdered form
- Water

Directions:

1. Mix together the water and salt. Channel positive energies into them as you charge the salt water mixture. Then add the powdered rosemary and powdered garlic into the water mixture.

2. Start at the very front of the house and make your way through the house by gently dripping dots of the water mixture around the home. Chant in a firm voice:

   "Evil must leave and will not re-enter."

3. Be very firm as you are speaking, don't leave doubt or fear. Slowly move through the house in a counterclockwise movement, repeating the dripping of the water and the commandment in every room, open door or window that needs to be protected. This spell can be repeated whenever you feel like it is necessary to bless and protect a house.

Chapter 3: Family and Wicca

Wicca does not have to be practiced solo or on your own. You can do it with the help of others, and you can practice it with your family as well. There is a history that exists behind the concept of being Wiccan and having Wicca in the family.

In this chapter we will just briefly explore what exactly that history can mean for some people and how Wicca plays a role in family bonds.

Wicca in the Family

The more you mingle in the community of Wicca, the more you will learn about familial bonds and how many Wiccan families practice Wicca as their religion. It is not as uncommon as one might think.

The same way that you can meet people whose entire family is Christian or Catholic and has been for generations, so too can you meet Wiccans who have a long history of family practice and belief. Sometimes you might even hear people refer to themselves as being a witch through their ancestry. This simply means that being Wiccan is all they have ever known and believed since birth.

While there are extremists (as there are in any religion) that do believe the ability to be Wiccan is born in their blood, this is not what is generally meant when people express their long family history with Wicca. There is no specific DNA strand that makes you more adept at Wicca or not. Just like you are not born as a Muslim or as a Catholic, you are not born as a Wiccan. However, when you are raised in an environment that practices and beliefs in the foundation of Wicca then you are more likely to grow up with Wicca as your religion.

So, while it may seem odd to hear someone say that they have been Wiccan since birth, it will generally just mean that they come from a family of practicing Wiccans. Yes, some people seem to have a better hand at Wiccan spells and practicing the magic, however that can be said for any talent in the world. It takes time, practice, dedication, and a true respect for what you are doing.

At the end of the day, it is not odd to be part of an entire family that practices Wicca, the same way it is not odd to be part of a family that practices Christianity.

Family Bonds and Magic

Family can be a tricky thing to maneuver. Whether you practice Wicca on your own or you are part of a family unit that has adopted the religion entirely, each family experiences their own trials and tribulations.

Wicca is not a cure-all for family drama, but being united in practicing a religion can strengthen some family bonds.

If you are the only Wiccan in your family, it can be daunting to come out and let them know what kind of belief system that you hold dear. This is particularly true for Wiccans who come from families who might not understand the Wiccan religion. The great thing is that there are so many different ways that you can communicate your beliefs to your family.

And, at the end of the day, if you just are not ready then you are not ready. I want you to make the best choice for yourself. Being open and honest with others about your journey through Wicca will only strengthen your personal spirit, but this can take time to work up to. Remember that Wicca is a journey and not an overnight transformation.

I can only hope that you are able to share your

connection to Wicca with other individuals. Being Wiccan in a family of Wiccans can come with its own set of challenges, but you can also feel the strengthening of bonds due to a shared belief system.

I do want to briefly point out that there is a big difference between practicing Wiccan families and practicing within a coven. I will go more in depth about this later on in this book.

The great thing about being Wiccan is that there are energies that you can visualize and spells that you can practice to strengthen family bonds. You can do this whether you are the only practicing Wiccan or your whole family practices. Wicca does not discriminate and you can often use your spells to help protect or nurture a relationship with someone that does not practice like you do.

Chapter 4: Covens

Covens seem like an easy concept to grasp, but there is often so much unknown about them within Wicca. Once you have a baseline understanding for what Wicca is, we can start to work on your more in-depth understanding about the intricacies of Wicca — covens make up part of that intricacy.

There is so much more to being part of a coven than just finding a group of people and joining them. As with every other choice you make in Wicca, this too is a personal one and being part of a coven is not a mandatory requirement. So, you can have freedom with your choice about how you practice Wicca and who you practice with. The goal of this chapter is to help guide you into making a more informed choice about being part of a coven.

Wiccan Covens

Coven is not a bad word, though the history books have tried to paint it as such. It is actually derived from Latin and its root meaning is "come together". In fact, during ancient times, coven was used not just exclusively for Wiccan gatherings, but for any celebration or gathering that was occurring amongst people.

It was not until the 1600s when the word coven started being associated with those who practice similar rituals as is done in the Wiccan faith. The use of the word coven was forgotten or barely mentioned until the mid-twentieth century when a Wiccan revival occurred.

So, what is a coven and what does it mean? As Wicca has evolved, so too has the meaning and shape of what a coven looks like. However, traditionally a coven consists of thirteen witches. These witches gather together to share their worship for their goddess and god and to practice their ritual magic.

In the days that have since gone past a coven was meant to have a High Priestess and High Priest. These positions were meant to symbolize the god and goddess that the coven worshipped. While these positions have fallen away in many of the new generation covens, there are still covens who practice with the original traditions. So, if you do want to join a coven that still observes the positions of high priestess and high priest then it is possible.

As mentioned earlier in this book, Gerald Gardner was considered the original founding father of the Wiccan covens as we know today. Along with Gardner, Alex Sanders was another prominent

Wiccan who had his own coven. There are covens that still exist in today's space that come from the covens during Gardner's and Sander's time. They have not forgotten their roots and they still hold tightly to them.

So, you see, even amongst covens there are differences. While some covens hold onto their values and beliefs from the time of Gerald Gardner, other covens have adopted new age beliefs. Instead of having positions of power, new-age covens have tried to implement a system where everyone feels justly heard and important to the functioning of the coven.

One of the traditions that most (not all, but most) covens still uphold is the need for a specific ritual in order to initiate any new coven members. The new coven member will need to understand how their coven operates, their belief systems, and the type of magic that they will be practicing. There is a great deal of preparation that goes into becoming a part of a coven, and this should not be taken lightly. Each coven will work differently, but they each have their own unique opportunities to grow in the craft of Wicca and to learn more about the intricacies that are still undiscovered in Wicca.

All Wiccans normally celebrate specific celebrations and solstices, and covens may convene to do the same. Which celebrations they adhere to will be specific to each coven, however, generally Esbats and Sabbats are observed by a coven as a whole.

If you join a coven, expect to form close and personal bonds with those that are in your coven. A coven is similar to a family and the bonds within it are meant to be strong, tied together with mutual beliefs and understanding.

Joining a coven is not like joining a church in which you worship your chosen god, or going to temple or even mass. This is a deeply personal journey and decision and it can either be a good thing for your energy or a bad thing. This is why you need to be careful with the coven that you choose to join and make sure that it is the best thing for everyone involved. While you may feel like your coven is interviewing you, you must remember that you are also interviewing them. Energies are important in Wicca, and you don't want to combine the wrong type of energies together because it could negatively affect you and the coven you are trying to join.

The other aspect of joining a coven is that when you do so, you are making a commitment. It is not just about you anymore. You are committing yourself to partaking in the rituals that the coven celebrates jointly. This means that your contribution will be expected and you cannot just skip out on this responsibility if you do not feel like it. Being part of a coven is a pretty serious commitment.

Covens can be tricky for a new Wiccan to navigate, and most newly introduced Wiccans will not join a coven as they are still getting to know the ropes. You will want to spend time learning and growing in your new faith before you seek out joining a coven. I would tell you to give yourself around a year of faithful study and practice in the Wiccan religion before you try and join a coven.

Of course, as this is a personal journey, you will decide how to go through your Wicca path with your own timeline. This might mean that you join a coven sooner rather than later or perhaps you might never join a coven.

I am about to throw another wrench in the works here by adding more information to the concepts of covens. There is more to Wicca gatherings than just covens, and you do not have to be part of a coven in order to find community in Wicca. That is why Wiccan Circles exist as well.

You might not want to dive into being a member of a coven, and that's okay. It comes with some pretty hefty responsibilities. Wiccan circles offer you a chance to find community amongst other Wiccans without the responsibilities of a coven. They are considered an informal gathering, and there are often no limits on the number of participating

Wiccans. You can benefit in various ways from a Wiccan circle, whether that is just to find a friend with a like-minded individual or if you want to learn more about the craft and practice.

The Sabbat and Esbat rituals are important to Wiccans, and while they may not be practiced in all Wiccan circles due to the informality, some circles do create celebrations amongst their peers for these rituals. In this case, unlike the coven, your attendance is completely optional.

You can start your own circle by simply reaching out into the community, or you can find one that is already established. A Wiccan circle also is a great place for beginners to learn more about the religion that they have adopted.

Some people prefer to avoid covens and Wiccan circles alike. That is a valid way to practice your faith as well. The lack of a physical community could be due to your personal preference or merely due to a lack of covens or circles close to where you live. Another great option for those who lack a physical community can be to find community through online forums. There are many different ways to reach out to other Wiccans online and still manage to practice your Wicca craft on your own.

How to Form a Coven

You might have decided that forming a coven is what you want to do. If this is the path you have chosen, then there are a few things you need to know before you jump in head first. Please remember that most beginners do not form covens or even join covens right away and there is a good reason for this. There is so much to learn with Wicca that you will find through your entire life's journey Wicca will be continuing to teach you so many things about its own secrets and nature's secrets. You need to take the time to truly learn the basics and master those before mastering a coven.

A great place to start is to join an already established coven or take part in Wiccan circles so that you can learn the ropes and see what it takes to establish and run a coven yourself.

When you start a coven, you don't want to have a huge influx of people right away. Remember that different energies feed off of one another. Start small. If you can get three to six people to agree to be in a coven with you then that is a good starting point. This way, if you ever find that you want to add more members then your coven will have the room to do so. Members of the coven might all be at different levels of learning or in their journey with Wicca, but you should try to gather members who are on the same understanding so the coven can grow together.

Reading books about Wicca can definitely help your coven grow together so you might want to get a copy of a certain Wicca practice book for everyone and read it together.

When you form your coven, you will want to establish a place where the coven will meet for their gatherings. This includes ritual gatherings. Most coven gatherings should take place outdoors so that each coven member can have open communication to nature. Public parks or hiking trails and gardens are a good place to do this. Once you have a place picked out, you and your coven need to set out a time to meet. Esbat rituals are common times for covens to gather together as they are celebrated once a month on either a new moon or a full moon.

Meeting times are flexible, however, and you can choose a different date to meet if that is more convenient for the members of the coven. A good rule of thumb is to try and meet once a month at minimum.

In the modern world of technology that we now live in, adding one another to social media or even exchanging numbers is a great way to communicate and stay in contact with one another when you are not meeting. It can also help with last minute details about rituals and monthly meet ups.

Once all of the smaller details are established, you need to decide what your coven is going to be doing or discussing during the gatherings. Food is a good starting point at bringing people together, so always have something available or take turns providing sustenance during the gathering. In a new coven, you can have everyone work on their Book of Shadows. This could help build the bonds in the coven as well as build each individual member's expertise in Wicca crafts. As you get more comfortable and familiar with one another you can practice your magic together as a coven and do certain rituals within your coven.

The reason that these rituals are important is because they strengthen coven bonds as well as each individual's connection to nature and the goddess and god. As mentioned before, you do not need to have a high priestess and high priest of the coven if you choose not to. It just depends on which traditions you want to uphold.

A great thing to do with your coven as well is to tailor your festivities to the different rituals you will be practicing and do something together, or create something together. At the end of the day I hope you are able to find community through Wicca no matter which path you choose.

Spells to Help Your Coven

Bond Together

You will need:

- A lock of each member's hair
- Red, blue and pink strands of thread.

Directions:

1. Draw a pentagram on the ground and then have each member of the group place their lock of hair in the middle of the pentagram. Recite this chant:

    "I will bond, will become one with the others, together we shall be one, so mote it be."

2. Mix the locks of hair together and use the three colors of thread to tie the hair together. Each group member must take a turn wrapping the thread around the hair. You will start with the red thread. As one, recite:

    "Through love, through our energy, we are one. We are together."

3. Then take the blue thread and take turns wrapping this around the hair and say:

   "Through peace, forever connected, through peace, forever joined. We are bonded."

4. Finally, with the pink string being wrapped around the hair say:

   "Through love, through honor, we are together. We are bonded. So mote it be."

5. Bless the hair that is now bonded together and bury it somewhere outside, a place close to where you have committed to meet with the other members in the group.

Acceptance

You will need:

- One white candle
- Rosemary oil

Directions:

1. This spell needs an altar and it works best if you and others set the altar up together. You will want to invoke the feminine goddess that your coven worships for help with this spell. While you are casting this spell, keep

the attributes of friendship, love, acceptance, and gathering at the front of your mind. Be careful with this and make sure that all you and the other members agree about who to invoke because you never want to invoke a deity that you are not familiar with.

2. Open the ceremony up by offering up to the goddess and saying your prayers. A good offering for help with acceptance is to include fresh sprigs of rosemary or to offer up fresh sweet pea flowers.

3. Place a hand on the white candle and bless it, anoint it with the rosemary oil. If there are several of you, make sure each person takes a turn blessing the candle. Then chant:

"Goddess within my heart and who controls love,

Goddess that is able to offer acceptance and blessings,

Help us now in this time of need,

Offer us the acceptance that I offer to others."

4. The chant must be repeated a total of nine times as you anoint the candle. Charge the

candle at the same time with positive hopes and thoughts of acceptance. Everyone needs to charge the right energies into the candle.

5. Place the candle on the altar and light it. Let the candle burn. Hold hands together, forming a circle around the candle and chant as one while you focus on the energy surrounding the candle:

"Goddess of mine and those before me

Assist us with this spell today,

Help us see one another and

Help others see us

Accept us through their own eyes

Help us find the values of

True friendship and acceptance

Allow us to greet all friends with love

Guide our souls and the spirits of others,

Allow us to convene together

Let us accept the uniqueness within us all,

with love and understanding.

So mote it be"

6. Let the candle continue to burn for just one hour. Once an hour has passed, blow the candle out gently. Remember not to use your fingers to extinguish the flame as this is considered incredibly rude and distasteful. It might take a couple of days for this spell to work but it will help with acceptance inside and outside of the coven.

Chapter 5: Your Personal Wiccan Journey

I stress a lot how personal your journey with Wicca is and should be. This is because as you are finding your way in Wicca, you will need to remember that not everyone's path looks the same. Differences are good, our experiences add value to the world, they do not take away from it.

Here is the thing, while Wicca is a religion it is still so different from conventional Western religions that most of us have been exposed to. In typical Western religions you are taught to accept first and learn later. Wicca does not ask for this blind acceptance. Instead, the Wicca religion encourages you to learn and make an informed decision about whether this is the right path for you. It gives you a true opportunity to sort through your beliefs. Depending on how a person learns, this impacts and influences their journey into the craft of Wicca.

Your Personal Journey

Before you go anywhere, before you claim to be Wiccan, before you even adopt any perceived belief system I advise you to read. Read, read, and read some more. If you feel like some of the concepts mentioned in this guide go above your head, go back to some beginner and basic books. Make sure that your foundation is secure before you start to build on it.

The general rule that most Wiccans go by is that when they started their journey into Wicca they studied it first for one year and one day. See if you can stick it out. But being Wiccan goes beyond just reading.

You need to decide what you believe (do you see where research plays a big role in making an informed decision?). What is your purpose for turning to Wicca? Remember that Wicca and witchcraft are not mutually exclusive, you can have one without the other.

Like other religions, Wicca has its own deities that its followers worship and draw strength from and you need to decide if you believe in the masculine god and feminine goddess as represented in Wicca.

You also need to understand that as a Wiccan you will pray to your gods and goddesses and worship them. You will ask them for guidance and strength. You need this to create a connection to something other than the physical world that we live in. If you struggle to pray then my best advice to you is to start with meditation. Meditation can open a lot of doors for you, and thankfully it pairs well with the Wicca religion.

Once you have made the decision to take the dive into Wicca, I suggest that you observe others practicing. Find a Wiccan circle, or even YouTube it. The internet can be a wealth of resources at times so, use all of the tools that are at your disposal.

Observing, however, goes deeper than observing those around you. Start being more aware of your connection to nature, the phases of nature. The moon is important to Wiccans, start learning the different phases and what they mean.

Slowly as you dip your toes into Wicca, begin building your altar and gathering tools that you want to use in your rituals. Start out small and build your collection overtime. Most importantly - never stop learning.

Wiccan Spells to Help You

Banish Thoughts

We have all had negative ideas and opinions form in our minds, sometimes this can interfere with our positive energies and our connection. You need to be able to clear your mind and here is just the spell to help you.

Ingredients:

- A black candle

Directions:

1. Hold your black candle in your hand and charge it with all of the negative energy inside you. The reason it needs to be black is because black will more quickly and thoroughly absorb the negative energy within you.

2. As you charge the candle with negative energy, meditate. Meditation will help you channel all of your negative feelings into the candle that you are holding. Allow everything that you are feeling to come to the surface, don't repress the negative emotions inside you. You want them to

come to the surface so that you can acknowledge them and then release them into the candle.

3. The candle should now be charged with the negative energy, and if you still feel residual negativity within you, continue to charge the candle until you feel all of your negativity leave.

4. Once you are done, place the candle on your altar and light it. Let it burn down all the way until the candle is finished.

5. As the candle burns, go back into a meditative state and focus on relaxing your body. Let every muscle relax as you feel the tension release. At this point you might find yourself exhausted, and that is normal. You just went through a lot of different feelings in a short span of time. If you need to nap, take one. Don't do this spell before bed because you need to give yourself time to enjoy the inner peace you should be feeling soon.

6. A walk through nature can be invigorating and is optional, but I recommend it after doing this spell. It can replenish energies that you spent in the spell. Embrace the positivity that you should now be feeling.

Dream Sweet

You will need:

- Warm water in a bowl
- Coarse salt
- Sprigs of rosemary
- Sprigs of basil
- white thread

Directions:

1. Dissolve the coarse salt into the bowl of warm water.

2. Tie the sprigs of herbs together using white thread and then dip them gently into the salt water mixture. Go into your bedroom and lightly sprinkle each corner in the room with the water. Make sure that you are using the sprigs to spread the water around the room.

3. Move to your bed and sprinkle more of the water mixture around the foot of your bed, the head of your bed, and also the blankets on your bed.

4. Once you have sprinkled the water, take the herbs and place them under your pillow or

under your mattress. If you place them under your mattress make sure that you keep them in the middle of the mattress. You should go to sleep that night and try your best to relax.

5. In the morning, grab the herbs that you slept on and bury them. It is best to find an area like a crossroad to bury the herbs, but if you cannot do this then crumble them up and let the wind carry them away from your house. The key though is to not let them settle around your home.

6. Once these herbs are gone, they will carry with them the negative energy and spirits both from your room and your bed. The use of rosemary and basil together helps with both protection and clarity as well as wisdom. You can add additional herbs if there are other requirements you need from this spell, but the focus should be on cleansing and purity. Your room should feel cleansed after this, but also your spirit and energy should feel uplifted.

Chapter 6: Intermediate Spells

I wrote this book for you based on the premise that you already have a fairly basic understanding of Wicca and its Craft. Again, I will suggest that if you feel out of your depth at any point while reading this book that you brush up on where you are feeling lacking in expertise. The reason is because you want to make sure that you are adept in your knowledge before attempting Wiccan Craft and magic.

The spells below are considered to be for those of an intermediate level who can manage the basic spells and are looking for a few more challenging spells to learn in their craft.

Intermediate Spells for Herbal Magic

Potion for Happiness

You will need:

- Two glasses of water
- A charged crystal
- Dried oregano
- Two sticks of cinnamon
- Star-anise
- Fresh sage
- Fresh catnip
- One teaspoon of honey
- Sachet

Directions:

1. Boil the charged crystal in the water on a stove top.

2. Gather together all of the herbs in a sachet and tie it together. Once the crystal is boiling in the water, add the sachet into the boiling water and turn the water off. Allow this to steep for at least five minutes.

3. Pour the honey into a mason jar and then once the water has steeped with the herbs, add this to the honey jar. Mix it well together and drink. You will find that your

ability to see and experience the happiness in life increases.

Shining Health

You will need

- Coriander Seeds
- A small cloth bag or sachet

Directions:

1. Go to your altar, or an area in nature that you consider sacred to yourself. You want to make sure that your energies are in the right place. Being in a quiet and sacred place can help you channel the energies that you need. If you have been experiencing negative energies then I suggest that in the sacred place you take time to meditate. Focus on white light coming into you and dispel the black energy with every exhale.

2. As you are coming out of a meditative phase and you are channeling the right energy, hold onto it. Face the east in your sacred place and recite the following chant:

   "Great Goddess, Overseer of life and the feminine,

Allow me to feel, allow me to receive

The true life force that flows through me

All of this, so that I may have everlasting health

I beseech you this favor Great Goddess.

So mote it be"

3. As you finish the chant, stretch your body up, all the while maintaining the energy that you need to hold onto in your aura. As you look up toward the heavens, visualize the image of white light coming down from the universe and swallowing you up in its glow.

4. Repeat the chant and the visualization three times exactly. Make sure you are in a calm place and that you do not get disturbed as you are practicing this chant and asking for health to come into your body.

5. As you let nature sink its healing powers into your body, focus on the positive. Do not let the negative interrupt your thoughts. Feel every part of nature from the wind to the sunlight, or the moonlight. Feel the Earth beneath you. Focus on your connection to nature as you complete your meditation.

6. Finally, run a warm bath and place the coriander seeds in the cloth and tie them together. Then let the bag of coriander seeds seep into your bath water. Take a relaxing bath inviting healing to you as you release your tension.

Bag of Health

You will need:

- Lavender flowers
- Fresh ginger
- salt
- Clove
- Cloth to make a bag, preferably velvet or satin
- mint leaves
- Red thread

Directions:

1. In the cloth of velvet or satin place the lavender, ginger, salt, cloves and mint leaves.

2. Using the red thread, tie the cloth together to form a makeshift sachet. Place the sachet next to your bed and when you wake up every morning breathe in the fragrance from the bag. Charge it with positive thoughts as you breathe in the herbs. Repeat this every morning until you feel healing come to you.

Intermediate Spells for Candle Magic

Candle Healing

You will need:

- Three blue candles
- A needle
- A place where you can find quiet
- This is a nighttime spell and must not be done before the sun sets.

Directions:

1. Using the needle, carve your name into the candles, or if you are doing this spell for

another person, carve their name into the candles.

2. Once marked with the name, place the candles in a triangle on your altar facing one another. Light the candles and chant:

"Healing light, Shine bright tonight

Allow this power, allow your power to be used to heal."

3. Repeat the chant three times as you stare into the flames of the candles and visualize healing energy emanating from them. Focus on the object of what or where you want to heal.

4. Allow the candles to burn down until they are about halfway finished and then blow them out. Remember to never snuff the candle out with your fingers. This spell should work fairly soon and provide you with the healing that you are seeking.

Strength Within

You will need:

- White candle
- Candle holder

- Olive oil
- Sage incense
- Salt

Directions:

1. Anoint the candle with the olive oil. Take your time and really focus on the strength that you want from this spell as you are anointing the candle.

2. Sprinkle the salt over and around the candle. Make sure that the entire candle is coated in salt, avoid covering the wick area, but the rest of the candle should have a salty coating.

3. Charge the candle with energies focusing on strength. Visualize coming through your obstacles and challenges without breaking down. Picture the candle as being your shining light through the darkness that you are engulfed in. Continue to charge it with this positive energy and thoughts of strength.

4. Put the candle into the candle holder and light it. Have the sage incense lit as well and placed next to the candle so that the aroma of the sage engulfs the candle. Let the candle burn until there is nothing left. You should

feel the inner strength building inside you as the candle burns down to nothing.

Healing Waters

You will need:

- Warm to hot water
- Silver candle
- Sandalwood oil
- Salt

Directions:

1. Take the silver candle and light it. Move it into the bathroom and place the candle close to where it will illuminate the bath area. Turn down the lights in the room and let the candle's light be the focus. In the light of the silver candle, run a hot bath for yourself. Once the bath fills up, sprinkle the salt generously into the bath and then add five drops of sandalwood oil into the water.

2. Remove all distractions and step into the bathtub. Relax in the bathtub and let yourself sink into the water. Allow it to soak into your skin and deep into your pores. As you relax, close your eyes and visualize the

sickness within you leaving your body. Picture this sickness as blackness that is seeping out of your pores as you are inviting health through the oils in the bath.

3. Once you feel as if the water is flooded with the black illness, drain the tub and let all of that unhealthy water flow away and down the drain. Chant as you watch the water disappearing:

"Let this sickness flow out and away from me

Into the water, away from my body and down into the sea.

So mote it be."

4. When you feel like you have gained strength and the tub is completely empty of all water then stand up in the tub and let clean water splash over you. A shower is the most ideal for this. If you are struggling with a particularly difficult sickness, repeat this bath as many times as is necessary for you to feel better and in good health.

Conflict Resolution

You will need:

- A white candle
- Piece of paper
- A pen
- A bowl that has been blessed
- Water
- Basil

Directions:

1. Charge the candle with your intentions to resolve the conflict that exists. This could be a conflict between you and someone else, or even something else. The bottom line is that you want to finish and resolve the conflict. So, charge the candle with your pure intentions. Then light the candle and place it on your altar.

2. On the piece of paper write down the source of the conflict or the name of the person involved in the conflict. Once this is written down, chant the following:

"Distress that lives within my heart

Distress that clouds my mind and soul

Stop this harm, of thee I beg

Water of life shall purify

With peace and love I sanctify"

3. Say the following incantation three times and then burn the piece of paper in the candle's flame. Drop the burned ashes into the blessed bowl. Have the water and basil mixed together in a separate bowl so that the water can become infused with the energy from the basil.

4. Once in the bowl, cover the ashes with the water that you have and then stir this into a paste. Take the paste that you have created and rub this paste on your temples, gently in a counterclockwise movement.

5. (If you do not have a blessed bowl it is easy to bless one. Simply take the bowl in both of your hands and imagine your energy moving from you and into the bowl in the form of a bright white light. Meditate on your intentions and desire for the bowl and pour them all into the bowl.) Once you have finished with this spell you must remember to wash the blessed bowl completely.

Wiccan Food Recipes

Food! It is the sustenance that keeps us filled and happy. As I have mentioned before in this book, most Wiccans do pay close attention to what they put in their bodies. This can mean that they make deliberate choices in the meat that they consume by making sure it is grass-fed and ethically raised, or they practice veganism and vegetarianism.

As you are aware by now there are several rituals and celebratory periods that Wiccans follow. Most of these rituals follow the cycles of the moon as the moon is incredibly important to Wiccans. Below are just a few recipes that you can use to help celebrate these rituals!

The recipes below are great to prepare during the Fall Equinox which generally occurs between the 21st to the 23rd of September.

Wisdom Bread (In the shape of a turtle)

Ingredients:

- Two teaspoons of dry yeast
- Two teaspoons of brown sugar (honey can be used as a substitute in this recipe)

- One cup of lukewarm water
- ¾ teaspoon of salt
- Two teaspoons of vegetable oil
- Two and a half cups of flour
- Four raisins (for the eyes)
- One egg
- Green Food Coloring

Directions:

1. Place the lukewarm water in a small bowl and dissolve the active yeast in it. Once the yeast is completely dissolved in the water, add in the sugar, oil and salt. Whisk this mixture together until it is well mixed.

2. Sift the flour and then fold it in to yeast mixture. Gently fold in the flour until the mixture becomes a stiff dough. When you can no longer fold the flour in anymore, place the dough on a surface that has been floured, dust the dough with more flour and knead it with your hands.

3. You knead the dough by continuously folding it in half and then pushing down into the dough with your palm. You want to

do this until the dough springs back after being gently poked.

4. Once it is finished being kneaded, shape the dough into a ball and put it in a bowl that has been greased. Sift flour over the dough and cover it. Give the dough thirty minutes to rest and rise.

5. Once the dough has risen, knead it down and make balls for the bread. You want to make balls for the shell, the head and the legs. Make sure your biggest ball is reserved to be the shell. Then, place these on a greased baking sheet. For the shell, mark into it a pattern of crisscross using a knife or other sharp tool.

6. Place two raisins in the head dough ball for eyes. Allow the bread to rise for thirty more minutes. As it is rising, preheat the oven to 375 degrees Fahrenheit.

7. Whisk together one egg, one tablespoon of water, and the green food coloring in a small dish. Brush this mixture over the shape of the turtle that you have formed and then bake it in the oven for twenty-five minutes. The dough should be a beautiful golden-brown color. This recipe should yield two turtles.

Pot Roast for the Harvest

I highly recommend that you use your own herbs that you grow for this recipe as it makes a huge difference in the energy created from the dish. Most Wiccans do have their own herb garden (if you don't already try and set one up) as having your own herbs on hand is helpful for spell casting as well.

Ingredients:

- 3.5lb roast of beef
- ½ cup of butter
- One yellow onion (diced)
- 2 stalks of celery (chopped)
- Two garlic cloves (diced)
- ¼ teaspoon salt
- ¼ teaspoon ground black pepper
- One bay leaf
- ¼ teaspoon dried parsley
- ¼ teaspoon thyme
- ¼ teaspoon rosemary

- Four potatoes, peeled and chopped into one-inch pieces

- two cups of French onion soup

- ½ cup of peeled and chopped carrots

- ½ cup of peas or broccoli (this is optional and to taste)

Directions:

1. I suggest that you use a dutch oven for this as it yields the best results. Place the roast inside the dutch oven and brown it over a medium heat. Use half of the butter to brown it and then set the roast aside. Preheat the oven to 325 degrees Fahrenheit.

2. Using the remaining butter, sauté the garlic, onion, and celery together for two to three minutes or until the onions become golden and soft.

3. Add in the thyme, bay leaf, ground pepper, and parsley into this onion mix and sauté for an additional minute. Once all of these ingredients are well combined, add the roast back into the dutch oven. Generously sprinkle the salt over the roast and add your two cups of French onion soup into the pan.

4. Place the roast in the oven and cook for four hours or until the meat is tender. If needed, baste the meat with the soup mix as it roasts in the oven. After four hours, add in the carrots and potatoes to the pot. Roast it for another 45 minutes until the potatoes are soft.

5. If you choose to add peas or broccoli, add them in after the potatoes have cooked for 45 minutes and let it simmer for another fifteen minutes in the oven. Serve the pot roast on its own, with some fresh bread or rice and enjoy! This makes six total servings.

Yule is another special time of year for Wiccans, and with special celebrations come other special recipes and staples that are always fun to bake with family, friends, coven, or even just those within a wiccan circle. Celebrations in the Wiccan community are always a good time to come together.

Salad for the Solstice

Ingredients:

- one cucumber

- one can of chestnuts

- Grated parmesan cheese
- A vinaigrette-based dressing
- chickpeas
- red and yellow peppers

Directions:

1. Wash all of the vegetables together and let them dry.
2. Slice the cucumber as desired and julienne the red and yellow peppers. Place the vegetables in a bowl and mix them together. Add in the chickpeas and chestnuts. Toss the salad and then add a vinaigrette-based dressing and parmesan cheese on top.
3. Let the salad cool in the fridge for at least one hour before you serve it. This will give you about 4-6 servings depending on how you make it.

Yule Time Mornings

Ingredients:

- Four cups of milk

- ¼ cup of white sugar (you can substitute in honey for a healthier alternative)
- One teaspoon of butter
- ¼ cup chopped almonds
- One cup of white rice (make sure you wash the rice well)
- ⅛ teaspoon of cinnamon
- ½ cup of heavy cream

Directions:

1. Heat the milk up slowly in a large saucepan. Be careful not to bring the milk to a quick boil, but rather slowly heat it until boiling. Mix in the butter and the rice into the boiling milk.

2. Turn the heat down and let the milk simmer with the rice. Cover it up with a lid and do not stir it while it is simmering. Allow the rice to simmer for roughly one hour, or until the milk is completely absorbed.

3. Transfer the rice mixture to a medium bowl and stir in the heavy cream and the almonds. Mix it until all the ingredients blend together well. This treat can be served in a bowl dusted with the sugar and cinnamon for an especially yummy treat!

Samhain is an important Wiccan celebration - in fact, it is often considered the most important of all celebrations. So, you will want to celebrate this time of year with some tasty recipes that were created in homage for this day.

Apple Pancakes for the Witching Hour

Ingredients:

- Two cups of flour (make sure it is sifted)
- Four tablespoons of baking powder
- One teaspoon of salt
- Two tablespoons of sugar
- Two eggs (separate the yolks from the whites)
- Two cups of milk
- Two tablespoons of melted butter
- One cup of apple (peeled, cored, and chopped finely)

Directions:

1. In a large mixing bowl mix together all the dry ingredients. Once mixed, sift them so that the mixture is well separated.

2. In a medium mixing bowl, mix together the milk and the two egg yolks. Add this into the dry flour mixture and combine the ingredients well. Add in the melted butter and the chopped apples.

3. Beat the egg whites until they are stiff and then fold them into the mixture that you have prepared. Allow the mixture to sit for ten minutes.

4. Heat up a griddle or frying pan. Once it is hot, pour the batter onto the griddle to cook the pancake. Use about ⅓ of a cup of batter for each pancake. If the batter is not spreading evenly, use your spatula to even it out.

5. Cook each pancake until golden brown on each side. Remove the pancake from the heat and garnish it with butter and some powdered sugar. Then roll it up and sprinkle cinnamon on top. Serve while hot. This should make between ten and twelve pancakes.

The Food You Use

These recipes may seem ordinary to you, but the reality is that each ingredient is deliberate and purposeful. Cooking in the Wicca religion can mean a lot and it can be as intricate and important as your spell work.

Kitchen witchery is a growing concept in Wicca, and it puts the kitchen right at the center of it all. When you create meals from scratch you are the one in control of what you are putting into your body and what you are nourishing yourself with. Everything from the Earth means something and has a purpose, when we cook with those same ingredients we are inviting and invoking the use of those ingredients into our lives.

So, how do you create a place of practicing magic in your kitchen? The first thing you need to do is clean and declutter your kitchen. This is a sacred place and so should be treated as such. If there is an abundance of dirty dishes it clutters the area up and prevents the flow of magic from you to the food.

If you want, you can also create an altar in your kitchen so that it is easy for you to combine those recipes that deal with both cooking and spell work in one.

Another excellent idea which I have already mentioned is to cultivate your own herb garden. This can even be as simple as dedicating a window sill to be the herb garden in your kitchen. Herbs are relatively easy to grow and keep alive, and nothing beats the freshness and energy you receive from growing your own. The staples are usually basil, rosemary, thyme, mint, and parsley. However, you can grow any combination that suits you. Think about the herbs that you use the most and then cultivate them in an herb garden. The benefit of this is that it will also help in your craft when herbs are required.

Energy is an important aspect of Wiccan craftwork. You use it in spell casting all the time. The same goes for your cooking! Whenever you cook, hold the ingredients that you are cooking with and charge them with positive energy. Think about what your intentions are as you cook and what you want to gain from the meal then put that energy into the food.

Are you curious about what some of your foods in the kitchen mean?

- Lentils - peace
- Oats - prosperity
- Rye - Fertility and love
- Beetroot - love, passion, and beauty

There are a host of things in your fridge and cupboard that you are cooking with that have specific uses in Wicca. While it can be a lot to learn, I highly recommend familiarizing yourself with the purposes for both herbs and food items. It can make a world of difference in how you cook and what you cook.

Wiccan Celebrations

There are many Wiccan holidays that are practiced and celebrating in today's time. These holidays are referred to as "Sabbats" and they correspond to the Earth's seasons and its own rhythms of nature. The purpose of the Sabbat is to celebrate the Earth as it travels around the sun.

The eight most popularly celebrated Sabbats are:

- Yule is also known as the winter solstice. This Sabbat occurs between December 20-23rd. Most Wiccans decide for themselves what the best day to practice and celebrate their Sabbat is. The Yule celebration falls on the day that has the longest night and the shortest amount of daylight. This normally signifies the ending of the year for Wiccans. The purpose of the Yule is to celebrate the return of longer days and shorter nights. This time of the year is when the sun is being reborn, and new beginnings and hopes are welcomed.

- Brigid's Day is celebrated on the 1st or 2nd of February. This ritual is the celebration of spring! During Brigid, Wiccans clean their living environments and organize their lives. It is a time to invite new things in. As Brigid is celebrated, Wiccans focus on cleansing their mental and emotional spaces as well. They want to grow and blossom in the coming seasons and so this is the time to prepare themselves for that growth.

- The Spring Equinox has many names such as Eostar and Ostara. It typically occurs between March 20th and the 23rd. The Spring Equinox means that winter is officially in the past and that the balance between day and night is equal for now. The idea that spring is on its way brings forth waves of fertility, birth and the concept of renewal. Also, this is where the growing season normally starts.

- May Eve is known as May Day and Beltane. You might be familiar with May Day as it is normally celebrated by many people alike, Wiccan or not. For Wiccans this day is normally on May 1st. During this season, marriages and unions are abundant as this is considered the time when the Goddess Mother Earth and the God of the

Greenwood celebrated their own union. The Beltane festival is a fertility festival that comes from centuries of practice. It is used to indicate that planting season has begun. It is supposed to be a light-hearted time that is filled with growth and joy.

- The Summer Solstice happens between June 20th and the 23rd. This is typically the longest day of the year, and the shortest night. Light wins over darkness during this time of the year. The preparation for crops before has now come to fruition and the signs of growth can be seen. The Summer Solstice is one of the most joyous celebrations as it brings with it light, laughter, and abundance.

- Lammas or otherwise known as Lughnasad happens on August 1st. In ancient times this celebration brought both fear and hope to the people. This was because the harvest was normally reaped during this time and it was always a fear that the harvest would not be enough to provide for everyone. Now, Wiccans in modern times use this season to focus on confronting their fears and creating a space for growth. They also make sure to protect their homes and those that they love. This would be a good time of year to renew protections over your home.

- The Fall Equinox is also called "Mabon". This season happens between September 20th and the 23rd. The light and the darkness are at balance again during this time as both the day and night share the time equally. Mabon is usually the time when the final harvest of the year was being done and the last bits of food were being brought for preparation of winter. This celebration is where Wiccans offer up their thanks to their deities as well as one another.

- Samhain is also known in the Wiccan community as Hallowmas or All Hallow's Eve. This is generally a celebration on October 31st. Normally this celebration is the beginning of a brand-new year and it is also one of the most important Sabbats celebrated by Wiccans. The ancestors get honored and remembered during this time and all of the year's accomplishments are celebrated at this time.

Conclusion

Thank you for coming through this guide and bringing it to a close. It has been a delight for me to write this book for you and create it for you. There is so much to Wicca that it can be a daunting process to learn it all, but if you take it one step at a time you will find it hard to remember a time in your life where Wicca was not second nature to you.

Through this guide I hope that you have come to understand the importance of self-care and that you need to take care of yourself before you take care of anyone else. You need to be in your best mental, physical, and emotional health. The spells I have provided in this guide are meant to help you achieve peace and protection.

As humans, we are easily stressed when life fails to go the way we want it to, and this can cause our problems to spiral out of control. Using meditative techniques, praying to the goddess and god, and making sure that you are taking care of your own needs are the first steps toward making sure that you are in the right mindset to tackle your problems.

Wicca has a deep and colorful history. Despite being a fairly new religion, Wicca has roots that span centuries, as far back as the first Pagan ancestors. There is so much to learn about how Wicca came to form into the religion it is today and the interesting battle with government authorities to get Wicca recognized as a religion.

Today, Wiccans enjoy much more religious freedom than they did in the past, as well as a more tolerable society. Where Wicca was once demonized, now it has come to light how it is a religion of acceptance and wisdom.

The other important part that this guide goes through is the difference between your family and your coven, because yes, there is a difference. Being part of a coven can completely transform your experience as a Wiccan, but it is definitely not a mandatory requirement to being Wiccan. There is so much community to be found, and I pray that you explore these different avenues so that you can find encouragement through individuals who understand your journey.

Please, I do implore you to remember that you do not have to practice magic to be a Wiccan, and you do not have to be a Wiccan to practice magic. Wicca at the end of the day is a religion, and it has its own set of beliefs, gods, goddesses and rituals. All of these should be respected and upheld by someone who is practicing the Wiccan faith. You need to decide for yourself what path it is that you seek to take.

Instead of being a religion of witches on broomsticks, Wicca is a religion that practices self-care, acceptance, and love. It is not a religion that seeks to create harm or evil in the world, particularly as Wiccans value all life and seek to improve the life for all beings on this Earth. Peace is synonymous with a practicing Wiccan. They embody the components of being peaceful, and that is what I pray you find through this guide.

Healthy eating is a major part of taking care of your own body. Treat it like a temple and it will reward you. I want you to remember that, and take pride in what you consume. There are some recipes in this book that will help give you an idea of some fun meals you can make during ritual celebrations. The important thing about preparing food is that it absorbs the energy that you put into it. It is helpful to make sure your kitchen is clean and your head is clear before you create food that you are going to consume.

Everything that you put out into this universe will touch the life of someone or some being. We are not exempt from our actions and our negative energies. I hope that you make good use of the spells within this book that help you manage and banish those negative emotions that might overwhelm you.

I am thankful that you are continuing your education in Wicca and that you are making informed choices about your personal journey. Good luck with all that this world has to offer you!

References

Editors, H. (2019). *Wicca*. Retrieved 23 July 2019, from https://www.history.com/topics/religion/wicca

Kopf, D. (2018). *The US witch population has seen an astronomical rise*. Retrieved 23 July 2019, from https://qz.com/quartzy/1411909/the-explosive-growth-of-witches-wiccans-and-pagans-in-the-us/

Wiccan spells. (2019). *How to form a coven - Wiccan spells*. Retrieved 23 July 2019, from https://wiccanspells.info/wiccan-pagan-articles/how-to-form-a-coven/

Sabbat food and recipes for wiccan and pagan celebrations. (2019). Retrieved 23 July 2019, from https://wicca.com/celtic/akasha/recipeindex.htm

Real magic spells. (2019). Spells - Real magic spells. Retrieved 18 July 2019, from https://www.spellsofmagic.com/spells.html

Wiccan covens, circles, and solitary practitioners. (2019). Retrieved 23 July 2019, from http://wiccaliving.com/wiccan-covens-circles-solitary/

Wiccans use self-care to enhance their lives. (2017). Retrieved 23 July 2019, from https://goddesshasyourback.com/2017/03/03/wiccans-use-self-care-to-enhance-their-lives/

Wigington, P. (2019). *What is a hereditary witchcraft tradition?* Retrieved 23 July 2019, from https://www.learnreligions.com/about-hereditary-witchcraft-2562544

www.ingramcontent.com/pod-product-compliance
Lightning Source LLC
Chambersburg PA
CBHW071021080526
44587CB00015B/2443